THE MANAGER'S KITBAG

New Words for Old Ideas

Garth Holloway

To order additional copies of this book, contact:
Xlibris LLC
1-800-455-039
www.xlibris.com.au
Orders@xlibris.com.au
521984

Acknowledgements

With thanks to:
Shamim Ur Rashid for the cover design;
Victor-Adrain Cruceanu for the graphics;
Stephany Aulenback for editing the book;
Charles, Kailash, and Venkatesh for their friendship;
and Russell Swanborough for informing so much of my foundation
thinking; and finally Amit Kumar Das for his unbelievable inspiration.

Dedication

To my late father with all my love.

Contents

Preface

Thank you for taking the time to read some or all of the articles contained in this collection.

This is the third in a series of three books. The first is a collection of longer articles on a selection of the common business concepts that a manager may be expected to encounter throughout the various stages of their career. The second is dedicated to the discipline of change management while this book is intended to be more practical and provides a range of tools and techniques for the manager's kitbag.

Each chapter is written as a stand-alone article, which requires that a number of the central concepts are repeated in the different papers. This has been kept to a minimum but could not be completely avoided.

Strategy Development Workshops

This article covers the basics of developing a business strategy. My favourite maxim on strategy management is "The bus that runs over the pedestrian is never the bus the pedestrian is watching." This maxim reinforces the point that the value of a business strategy is directly related to the assumptions that underpin it.

When establishing a strategy, the first assumption is that the management team formulating the strategy all frame the conversation the same way. Invariably this is not the case and the book "Reframing Organisations" by Boleman and Deal describes this phenomenon very well.

In their book, they describe four frames through which a manager can view the organisation and environment they work in.

- **The structural frame:** a focus on how groups and teams are structured.
- **The human resource frame:** a focus on human resource management and positive interpersonal dynamics.
- **The political frame:** a focus on power and conflict, coalitions and dealing with internal and external politics.
- **The symbolic frame:** a focus on organisational culture.

Recognising that managers may not be aware that they view the organisation differently as do their colleagues, it is important to agree the frame or frames the team will use through the strategy development process. It is acceptable that different managers explicitly adopt different frames to enrich the conversation and ensure groupthink is mitigated. It is only important that everyone knows which frame each person is using through the course of developing the strategy.

The strategy management process is depicted as follows:

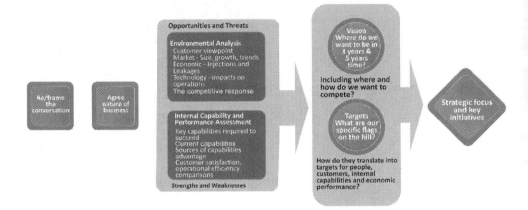

Simplistically, the purpose of a strategy workshop or process is to answer five questions:

1. What business are we in?
   a. What is the corporate culture?
   b. What is the risk appetite?
2. What is the endgame or, in other words, what does success look like?
   a. Asset sale
   b. Public listing
   c. Family business hand-down
   d. Stop investment and take the money in annual dividends.

3. Why will we succeed?

    a. Analysis of the operating environment

    a. How is value created?

    b. Who are the competitors?

4. How will we succeed?

    a. S.W.O.T. analysis

    b. What is the business model?

    c. What is the style and structure of management?

    d. What are the priorities?

5. How will we manage success?

    a. Organisation structure

    b. Compliance management

    c. Performance management

The strategy workshop should open with confirmation of the nature of the business, the company culture, and the risk appetite. The nature of the business is to answer the question: "What business are we really in?" Often the answer will revolve around business models such as treasury or risk. These models are then placed in the context of the business they operate in. For example, supermarkets are generally in the treasury business and construction companies are in the risk business. Understanding the company culture will inform the strategy process as to the nature of the risk the company is willing to take on. For instance, a conservative company will not endorse a high risk strategy.

It is difficult to develop a strategy if there is no consensus on the nature of business, culture and risk profile.

The strategy workshop can now move to an analysis of the endgame. The purpose is to establish agreement on the exit strategy. The exit strategy is a statement of how the owners will turn their investment in the asset into cash. Options include: sell it, list it on the stock exchange, or take the cash in billings without actually building the asset. An equally acceptable option is to give it to the kids.

The endgame question informs the investment decision. For example, it is very difficult to sell a professional services business and if the principles wish to exit the business, then investing in the business may not be the best way for them to get value from it. Rather they should maximise their billing and take out the value in dividends over the next few years, then simply close the business and walk away.

The endgame question is equally valid for a public company, but the alternatives are different. There is only one objective for the directors of a public company and that is to maximise shareholder value. This reduces the directors' endgame to the alternatives of selling the entire company or selling the shares they hold in the company. There are a few additional complex options that are not included in this article.

If the business is saleable, or it is a public company, then the exit strategy will always be to sell the shares for the highest value possible. The business strategy must therefore focus on activities that increase share value in a sustainable manner.

The longest practical time horizon for a strategic plan is three years and many would argue that this is too long, but this depends on the market the company operates in. Developing a three-year strategic plan does not imply that the owners will exit in three years. The time frame is only to provide context for the strategy workshop and if the strategy development process is conducted annually, then the three years becomes a rolling three years. For some markets such as infrastructure development, the investment period is well over ten years.

At the beginning of this article I mentioned the need to manage assumptions. Through the course of agreeing the endgame, a number of explicit or implicit assumptions will have been made and the next stage of the workshop is to expose and critically examine these assumptions and answer the question: "Why will we successfully achieve the endgame?"

The intent of the question is to force an examination of the assumptions made about the market the business operates in (external environment) and the business's ability to operate in that market (internal capabilities).

There is no right or wrong order in which to approach these two mini workshops. My experience is that workshop participants need to discuss their internal environment before they can properly consider the external environment. The problem with this approach is that it can become very myopic and the thinking becomes constrained to considering what is known, rather than including what is unknown. If the workshop sequence does start with an analysis of the internal environment then it should include a reconfirmation of the results after the external analysis concludes. This will ensure the capabilities considered in the internal analysis adequately address the opportunities and threats identified through the analysis of the external environment.

For the internal analysis workshop to be successful it is important that there is agreement on the core business. That is agreement on the question: "What business are we in?"

Understanding what business you are in, tells you what you must be competent in and, by inference, what the business must be capable of. Many capabilities create a competency.

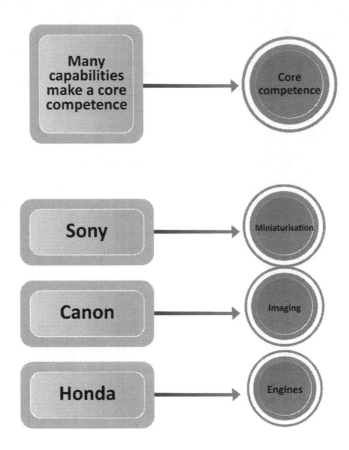

Source MGSM

The internal analysis is therefore a review of the existing capabilities against the nature of the business. It is a review of what exists now and what capabilities need to be introduced or enhanced. To guide the identification and classification of capabilities I recommend the B.T.O.P.P. model. It is a simple but practical model for structuring the analysis.

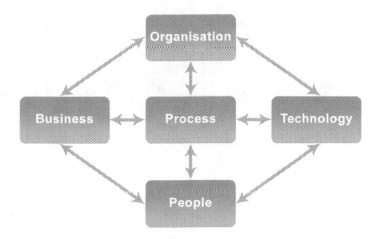

It is important to keep the analysis at a high level to avoid getting mired in conversation on the nitty-gritty. The following table provides a good structure for collating the results.

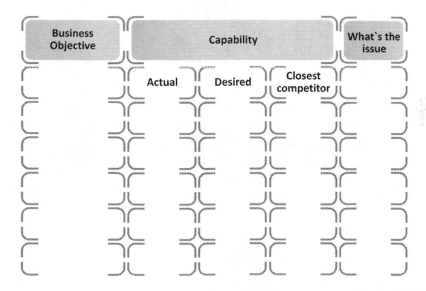

Source MGSM

Column A can be renamed "business objective" or "core competencies" or similar. The last column is important. It captures the group's opinion on what needs to be resolved to close the gap. I recommend using the B.T.O.P.P. model here again to check for completeness. This is in addition to using it for the capabilities analysis. For example, if the desired capability is to be able to establish a "multi-local" distribution chain or to be capable of transacting in multiple currencies, then the issues will be multi-faceted. Using the B.T.O.P.P. model creates a common vocabulary for recording the issues.

There are many models that assist with the analysis of the external environment such as Porters Five Forces (shown below), the P.E.S.T. (Political, Economic, Social and Technological), and P.E.S.T.E.L. (PEST + Environmental + Legal) frameworks.

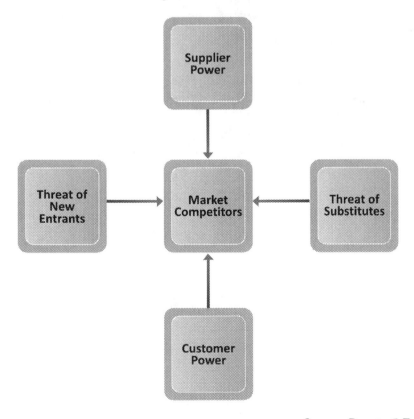

Source: Porters 5 Forces

The results of the analysis can be captured in a table as shown.

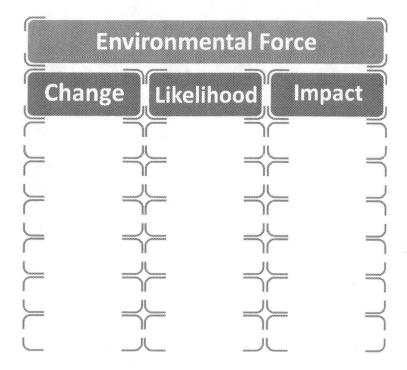

Environmental Force		
Change	Likelihood	Impact

Column A describes the nature of change anticipated in the market. While the table is simplistic, care should be taken to include as much detail as possible when describing the anticipated change. This may require adding additional columns. Depending on the depth of the analysis, a different table may be used for each analysis topic, or one table for all. The table is intended only to collate the issues, not to solve them so there is no column for mitigation actions.

The internal and external analysis addressed questions 3 and 4 (referred to at the start of the chapter) and provided the raw data required to answer question 5. The workshop is now ready to consolidate the issues and prioritise the actions for the next 12 months, 3 years, 5 years etc. The critical issues framework can assist with this process.

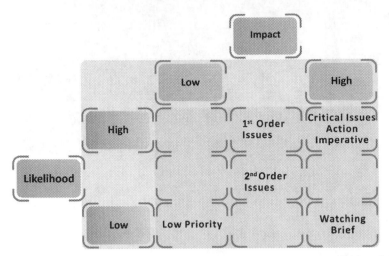

Source MGSM

The methodology is to use the grid to "sift" the issues gathered through the two analyses to determine the critical issues. It is important to treat the grid as a "relative" analysis in the sense that all the issues are important, but some are more important than others. This means that you should be able to place an issue in all nine cells. Placing an issue in the low priority cell does not mean it is not important. It only means that, of the raised issues, it is of a lower priority.

The critical issues are then further analysed as shown.

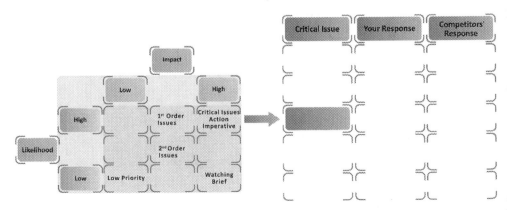

Source MGSM

The final step in order to conclude this stage of the workshop is to perform due diligence. The approach is to cross-reference the priority actions captured in the previous table to the business objectives discussed at the start of the workshop, or the required competencies highlighted through the capabilities workshop. Using a simple light/dark analysis provides an easily understood summary. Dark shading represents a closer match between the objective and priority.

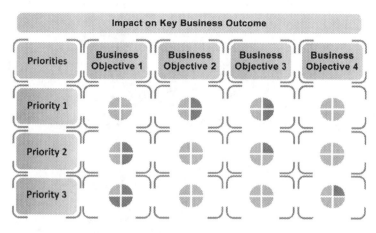

Cross-references that are overly dark should be examined for completeness. Is the underlying issue fully described and understood? Is the priority correctly applied?

The priorities are then associated with a high-level timeline and the workshop is now ready to answer question 5: "How will we manage success?"

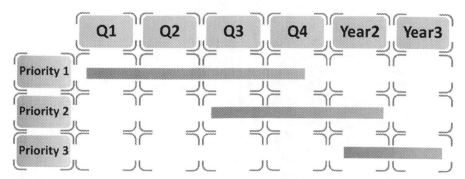

On the basis of "a journey of a thousand steps starts with the first step," the purpose of question 5 is to ensure there is agreement on the tactical changes or projects required to execute the strategy. The timeline provides the priority.

I close with the observation that managers frequently do not allow enough time for everyone to fully consider the points being discussed. The commonly heard statement is, "Let's just get something down on paper and we can refine it over email." This approach may improve efficiency but it destroys the debate. It is recommended that each activity in the workshop is addressed twice, if not three times. If it is a two-day strategy session, then repeat Day 1 on Day 2 to give people overnight to really think about the issues. Then hold a further review a week or two later.

Business Outcome Management

One of the greatest challenges for any company is the execution of strategy or the realisation of benefits from the implementation of large change programs. Frequently, the reason isn't organisational resistance to change, a difficulty that is commonly referred to. Rather it is for a more serious reason: managers and management teams focusing dogmatically on what they are doing rather than what they want to achieve. This causes managers to narrow their thinking and, in effect, operate at a more junior level. They "can't see the wood for the trees" and the return on investment from their time is diminished.

The more senior a manager, the more they need to work within a team to achieve the business objectives. Irrespective of how siloed the organisation is, the silos have to come together eventually. The lower in the organisation that this cross-departmental engagement occurs, the better.

A major inhibitor to cross-departmental engagement is the absence of common purpose. Frequently managers believe they are working cooperatively but when pushed they have difficulty explaining the interdependencies between the initiatives they are all working on. This is because they are working towards completing initiatives, rather than delivering outcomes.

Initiatives are the activities managers and staff are engaged in. Outcomes are the result of one or more initiatives.

Consider the technology salesperson. Their role is to approach prospective customers and convince them that their technology solution will improve the prospects' business operations.

For example, a CRM (customer relationship management) salesperson will state, "Buy my CRM software and you will have happier customers and improved revenues."

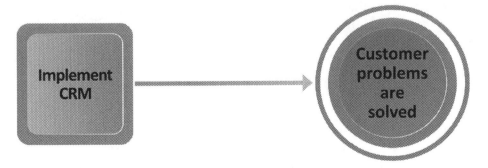

Anyone who has implemented a major piece of software will know how flawed this scenario is. The truth is that once you implement a technology solution, all you have is a database of names and files.

To achieve the benefits promised by the CRM salesperson, the company must implement a range of complementary initiatives. The collective output of these initiatives will deliver the desired outcome.

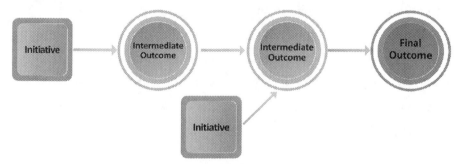

The approach of interlinking initiatives and outcomes is known as Business Outcome Management. It is fundamentally different from traditional approaches to project planning in that the emphasis is almost entirely on the outcomes required.

The principle is the same as it is for ball sport players in the sense that it is better to be where the ball is going to be rather than where it is.

Business outcome management is a methodology that assists management teams to establish a common purpose. It produces two deliverables. The first is a two-dimensional mind map that graphically displays the outcomes and initiatives and the second is a document that transposes the map into a business plan.

The importance of having a two-dimensional mind map cannot be overestimated. When discussing the importance of business outcome management with my clients they generally point to a range of documents or a single thick document and say they have it covered. At this time I ask them what the relationship is between their various documents, or how page x relates to page y in a single document. The point is that documents are "three-dimensional," making it exceptionally difficult to know or visualise the multiple many-to-many interrelationships that exist in a single document, and between documents.

A two-dimensional mind map surfaces the interrelationships and explicitly reveals how a single business outcome is dependent on multiple initiatives. It highlights relationships that are not immediately obvious in a document. The following is a simple example of the concept. Initiatives are represented as a square and outcomes as a circle. Risks can be included as a different shape.

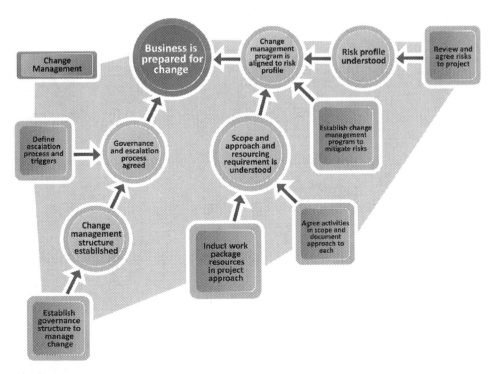

The graphic details the basics of implementing a change program. The entire "island" is labelled change management.

For larger projects and programs of work, the map will comprise of multiple "islands," each representing initiatives and outcomes of similar intent and strategic focus. They provide an additional dimension to the map and assist the process of aggregating the relationships found in traditional documents into an easier-to-read format. Each "island" is labelled to provide context for the outcomes within the island, and collectively these labels are the executive summary of the program of work. Each island will have its own owner, a manager who is responsible for ensuring all the outcomes in the island are achieved.

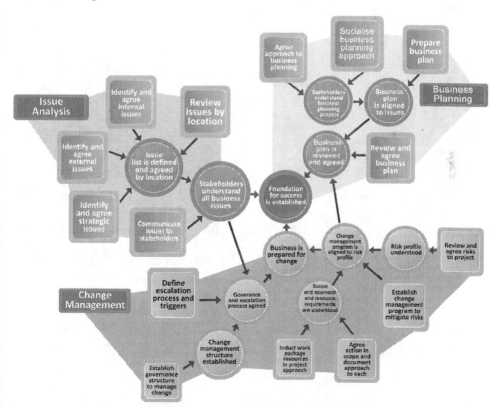

Initiatives are written in the format: verb/noun. For example: "document the business process" or "administer a customer survey." Outcomes are written in the past tense. "Staff morale has improved" or "customer requirements are understood" or "shareholder value has increased." Using the past tense is important as it assists managers to clearly articulate the desired outcome.

Focusing on achieving the outcome encourages the manager to avoid tackling a project with a checklist mentality, as it is almost impossible to document all the initiatives required to achieve an outcome.

If you were focusing on initiatives you would work on "review and agree upon the business plan" and once completed you would consider that the business plan was reviewed and agreed.

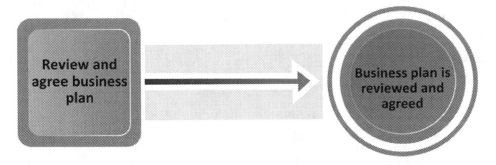

However, if you take a broader view, then you could only consider the business plan to be "reviewed and agreed upon" once all the indirect contributing initiatives were taken into account.

The indirect initiatives that contribute to "business plan reviewed and agreed" are:

- Induct work package resources in project approach
- Agree activities in scope and document approach to each

- Establish change management program to mitigate risk
- Review and agree risks to project
- Agree approach to business planning
- Socialise business planning approach
- Prepare business plan
- Review and agree business plan

These initiatives are part of two different strategic groupings (islands) but they all still contribute to the outcome and the manager who is signing off the business plan will expect to see contribution from all of those initiatives.

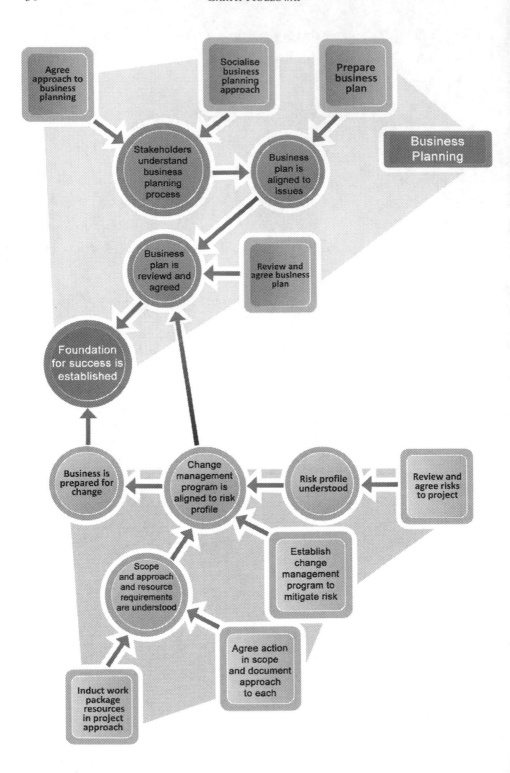

An important insight is that if a decision is made to delete or not complete an initiative, the impact of its absence can now be traced to those outcomes that relied on the initiative being successfully completed.

To prepare a business outcomes roadmap requires a workshop of four parts.

Part one is to agree the "endgame"—the flag on the hill. This is the medium-to-long term objective for the company or, if it is for a major project, then it is a statement of what the project will achieve. It should be a "big statement" but equally one that is achievable.

Example: "A culture of delivering excellence is implemented and a collaborative unified management team that is the envy of the industry is established."

The second part of the workshop is to discuss the current issues facing the business. This is because managers and staff frequently cannot discuss the future without first explaining the problems they face in doing their job. You have to give them the chance to "put their baggage down."

Part three of the workshop is to capture intermediate outcomes, those outcomes that must be realised in order to achieve the endgame.

Part four is to capture the initiatives collectively required to deliver the sub-outcomes.

The methodology for collecting the data is important and it starts with the room selected for the workshop. The room should be set up without a table and the chairs should be arranged in a semicircle or similar. This assists people to "open up" in the workshop.

Each person is given a felt-tip pen with a broad point and a pack of post-it notes.

Part one of the workshop can be completed on a white board through normal facilitation techniques.

Parts two to four will follow the same approach. The facilitator requests that the participants write one issue, outcome, or initiative (depending on the session) on a post-it note and to keep producing post-it notes until they have exhausted everything they have to say on the topic.

While the participants are writing down their thoughts, the facilitator should walk between them collecting the completed post-it notes and placing them randomly on a wall or window. As the notes are placed, the facilitator should read aloud a selection of the notes. This will stimulate the thinking of the participants.

When everyone has written down everything they have to say, and the facilitator has stuck all the notes on the wall, then the participants will be asked to sort the notes into groups. The rule for this part of the workshop is that the participants must work in silence. They cannot discuss their thoughts on the grouping. Once everyone is happy, the participants take their seats. At this time the facilitator will review each group and agree on a title for the group. These groups will later influence the "islands" in the mind map.

When all three mini workshops are complete, the workshop is over.

The facilitator types up the workshop and prepares the business outcomes mind map. This will include de-duping the lists. The issues list does not make the map. Rather it is used to validate that everything that is included in the map will address the issues. Microsoft Visio is a good application for preparing the mind map.

An important feature of this approach is that the outcomes are collected independently of the initiatives. This means there is no direct link between the outcomes and initiatives. When the map is prepared, the author must draw their own conclusions on which initiatives are related to which outcomes.

Once the map is prepared, it is critiqued by all or a subset of the participants from the original workshop. It may take two or three iterations until the map is agreed upon by all.

Viewing the map for the first time can be quite confronting for the participants. The best personal example of this was when I presented a map to a group of executives in the aviation industry. When they first saw the map, the room descended into chaos as each manager tried to find their department or function in the map. When they couldn't, they turned on me. I explained that each of their functions was spread out through the map and that they had to work as a team to deliver the endgame. It was a significant moment and once the emotion died down, they really embraced the concept. Later the managing director wrote to me to say that they were 27% up on the budget as a direct result of the workshop. He was ecstatic.

Once the map is agreed upon, it needs to be turned into a document. This document has two parts.

Part 1 focuses on outcomes and part 2 on initiatives. The layout is as follows.

For outcomes:

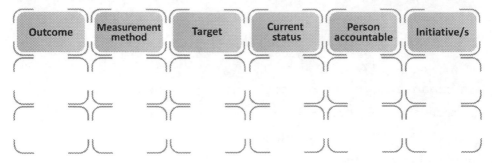

The idea is to list all the initiatives that contribute directly or indirectly to each outcome. The "person accountable" refers to the outcome, not the initiatives.

For initiatives:

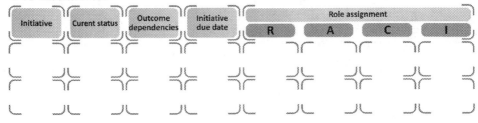

This table relates all outcomes to a single initiative. This is important as it informs the owner of the initiative about which outcomes are dependent on their activity being successfully completed. The R.A.C.I. table describes who will own the initiative (accountable), who will deliver the initiative (responsible), who will contribute to the delivery, and who should be informed of progress.

This is a powerful methodology and the results will improve with practice.

Driving Change—
A Methodology

Implementing change is difficult. Implementing change without a methodology is very difficult. This article will discuss the basics and provide a structure to guide your projects. It will have sufficient detail to be a stand-alone article, but when used in conjunction with all three books in the series "Old Words for New Ideas," it will definitely come alive and you will have all the models and structure you need to deliver a successful business improvement project.

The methodology comprises seven steps. It is important to note that while they are broadly sequential in nature, it is common for two or more steps to be tackled concurrently. This is particularly true for steps **4a** and **4b**.

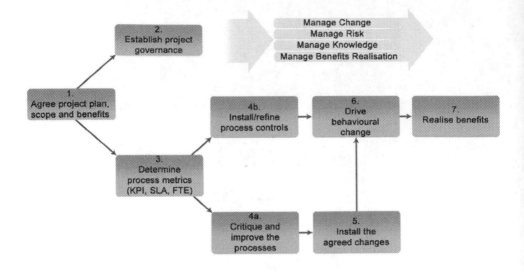

Step 1: Agree project plan, scope and benefits.

This is a crucial step in successfully establishing a project. Taking the time to get it right will provide a positive return on investment through minimising scrap, rework and failure.

Typically the focus of this step is the preparation of a document describing the project. These documents are normally termed Statement of Work (SOW), Project Initiation Document (PID), or Project Memorandum. Irrespective of the name they include the same generic contents:

- Business context
- Project purpose
- Scope
- Methodology
- Approach
- Timeline

- Risks and risk management
- Change management
- Staffing
- Roles and responsibilities

Depending on the author and company, additional headers may be included such as budget, success measures, related projects, and a methodology for handling change requests. Traditionally the project manager is asked to prepare the SOW and the document is then presented to the project sponsor and other stakeholders who review and approve it.

The biggest issue with this approach is that the focus is always on the document rather than what it represents; and it is typically always written in a hurry, often within a week. The sponsor reads the document and validates that all the information you would expect to see is there and that the timeline and budget are within bounds of acceptability and then accepts the document.

What is seldom done is for the stakeholders to formally put aside time to workshop the completed SOW to subject it to a rigorous level of due diligence. This workshop should ask questions such as:

1. Is there a common understanding of the project purpose? Even if there is a purpose statement, does everybody interpret it the same way?
2. Is there agreement on what success looks like?
3. Does each stakeholder understand and accept what is expected from them throughout the course of the project and more importantly, after the project?

4. Is the risk table complete? Does it include project and business risks? Are the mitigation strategies considered practical or are they merely a cut-and-paste from the last statement of work?

5. How will risks be managed? Merely writing them into the SOW is not managing them.

6. Is the change management plan aligned to the risk plan?

7. Does the resource plan make sense?

8. Does the budget have contingency? How is it calculated?

The sponsor should allow ample time for this workshop. The desired outcome is confidence that the project is considered and that the stakeholders are fully enlisted in the project. Not just engaged, but enlisted. That is, they are fully and actively committed to its success.

Step 2: Establish project governance.

The due diligence workshop is the first activity in establishing active project governance. Governance is the active mitigation of risk through the proactive management of compliance and performance. Merely to be in business requires the acceptance of a degree of risk. This is no different when embarking on a business improvement project.

Good governance requires the establishment of a hierarchy of committees to manage the project. I have covered these committees in detail in my two other books so I will be brief here.

The phrase "change management" is freely used on all projects. The reverse, "the management of change," is not. There is an important distinction between the two concepts and it is frequently overlooked. Frequently committee members attend project meetings, participate in discussions, and then mentally park the project in the back of their mind until the next meeting rolls around. They forget that their role is the active management of change and this requires a substantially higher level of involvement than merely attending a weekly project review meeting.

I suggest that change is managed through a three-tier structure.

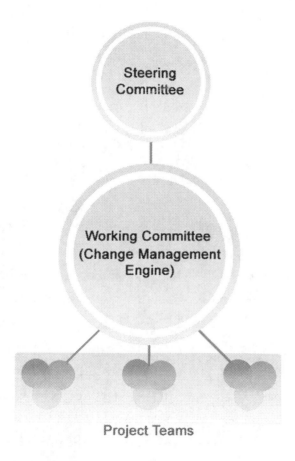

Project Teams

The steering committee is a group of senior managers responsible for ensuring the overall change program stays on strategy. A key point is that there should only be one steering committee. They are specifically responsible for steps **1** and **7**.

The working committee is responsible for driving the tactical change initiatives. There may be two or more working committees depending on the size of the company and the breadth of change. The working committee is specifically responsible for **step 6**. The steering committee is to ensure that their collective output will meet and promote the company strategy.

Both committees can manage risk, budget, and change, the difference being the scope of authority.

The project teams are responsible for the day-to-day delivery of the project activities represented by steps **3, 4** and **5**.

Step 3: Determine process metrics.

The purpose of step 3 is to collect and analyse primary data. Typically this step involves mapping the business processes. The step is termed "determine process metrics." This is an important label in the sense it does not say "business process mapping" as is frequently the case with business improvement methodologies. The essence of this distinction is that it is equally or more important to understand the metrics *behind* the process than it is to understand the process itself. A methodology to calculate these metrics is covered in the chapter on process reengineering.

These metrics should be seen in the context of the unit of measure for the process. This step could produce a table as shown.

	The number of variations by which a single item could be processed		The working hours expressed in minutes		The average unit cost		The annual transaction cost for the process		
		Unit Time				Annual			
Process by Function	Paths	Work (h)	Elapsed (m)	(d)	Unit$	Vol.	C..l.	FTE	Cost%
BUY									
PURCHASING	14	3.2	194	0.5	$144	3,936	$449,806	7.31	18%
RECEIPTS	28	0.4	26	0.5	$7.79	30,00	$233,700	7.47	9%
ACCOUNTS PAYABLE	63	0.6	35	1.0	$56	2,400	$134,520	0.81	5%
MAKE									
PICKING	18	1.1	68	2.0	$31	8,000	$246,560	5.20	10%
ASSEMBLY	102	1.8	105	2.3	$112	850	$95,591	0.86	4%
DISTRIBUTION	8	1.6	96	4.4	$361	895	$323,096	0.82	13%
INVOICE PROCESSING	17	0.3	15	0.4	$6.57	37,000	$243,090	5.44	10%
SELL									
CATALOGUES	14	25.0	1500	10.0	$51	6	$305	0.09	0%
MARKETING	3	6.0	360	30.0	$18.99	1,000	$18,990	3.45	1%
INVOICE PROCESSING	7	0.5	30	1.0	$18	100	$1,717	0.03	0%
IT MANAGEMENT									
USER ACCESS CONTROL	12	0.3	15	4.0	$7.80	25,000	$195,000	3.59	8%
ENQUIRY MANAGEMENT	11	0.9	56	0.2	$53	1,936	$102,724	1.04	4%
NEW USER SETUP	18	0.5	30	4.0	$20	21,600	$437,832	6.21	18%
					P% factor	00% l.'%	$2,482,990 $2,921,165	42.30 50	100%

Elapsed times are very conservative. Lower end estimates have been used throughout.

The average days elapsed to process a volume of 1 (drives customer service)

The annual transaction volume through this process

The full time equivalent staff requirement

In terms of benefits realisation, this table can be used to calculate the benefits and priority of the change to be addressed in step **4a**.

Step 4a: Critique and improve the process.

Once you have established the process flows and associated metrics for the current mode of operation, you are in a position to determine improvements to the processes. The data will guide the analysis and quantify the benefits of change. Without this data, it is difficult to confirm that any of the recommendations tabled will result in a substantial improvement. Different is not an improvement.

Business improvements can be achieved from changes associated with people, process or technology and any of their sub-components. The following table illustrates the primary sources of change.

Frequently improvement requires changes to more than one component.

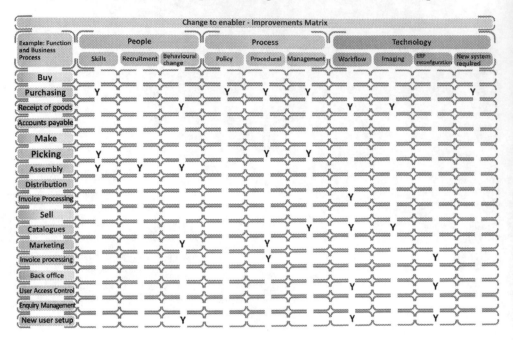

Example: Function and Business Process	People			Process			Technology			
	Skills	Recruitment	Behavioural change	Policy	Procedural	Management	Workflow	Imaging	ERP reconfiguration	New system required
Buy										
Purchasing	Y			Y	Y	Y				Y
Receipt of goods			Y				Y	Y		
Accounts payable										
Make										
Picking	Y				Y	Y				
Assembly	Y	Y	Y							
Distribution										
Invoice Processing							Y			
Sell										
Catalogues						Y	Y	Y		
Marketing			Y		Y					
Invoice processing						Y			Y	
Back office										
User Access Control							Y		Y	
Enquiry Management										
New user setup			Y				Y		Y	

Once you have worked out your business improvement strategies, you can quantify the benefits of change by determining the impact of the change on the same base data set from **step 3.** The results can be tabled as follows.

Current Mode of Operation

Process by Function	Paths	Unit Time Work (h)	Elapsed (m)	(d)	Annual Unit$	Vol.	Cost	FTE	Cost%
BUY									
PURCHASING	14	3.2	194	0.5	$144	3,936	$449,806	7.31	18%
RECEIPTS	28	0.4	26	0.5	$7.79	30,00	$233,700	7.47	9%
ACCOUNTS PAYABLE	63	0.6	35	1.0	$56	2,400	$134,520	0.81	5%
MAKE									
PICKING	18	1.1	68	2.0					
ASSEMBLY	102	1.8	105	2.3					
DISTRIBUTION	8	1.6	96	4.4					
INVOICE PROCESSING	17	0.3	15	0.4					
SELL									
CATALOGUES	14	25.0	1500	10.0					
MARKETING	3	6.0	360	30.0					
INVOICE PROCESSING	7	0.5	30	1.0					
IT MANAGEMENT									
USER ACCESS CONTROL	12	0.3	15	4.0					
ENQUIRY MANAGEMENT	11	0.9	56	0.2					
NEW USER SETUP	18	0.5	30	4.0					

Future Mode of Operation

Paths	Unit Time Work (h)	Elapsed (m)	(d)	Annual Unit$	Vol.	Cost	FTE	Change Cost	FTE
4	1.7	102.7	0.4	$62	3,936	244,032	3.87	-$205,744	-3
7	0.3	15.6	0.3	$4	30,00	$120,000	4.48	-$113,700	-3
12	0.4	24.5	0.5	$18	2,400	$43,200	0.56	-$91,320	0
12	0.4	24.0	0.5	$16	8,000	$128,000	1.84	-$118,560	-3
16	0.9	52.7	1.5	$49	850	$41,650	0.43	-$53,941	0
5	1.0	60.0	2.0	$98	895	$87,710	0.51	-$235,385	0
4	0.2	10.8	0.1	$4	37,000	$148,000	3.81	-$95,090	-2
4	0.8	45.0	3.0	$43	10,800	$464,400	4.66	-$464,095	-5
3	3.0	180.0	10	$12	1,000	$12,000	1.72	-$5,990	-2
2	0.1	8.0	0.4	$7	100	$700	0.01	-$1,077	0
4	0.0	1.0	0.1	$2	25,000	$39,000	0.24	-$156,000	-3
4	0.5	31.4	0.1	$16	1,936	$30,976	0.58	-$71,748	0
6	0.5	31.7	0.2	$11	21,600	$237,600	6.55	-$200,232	0
P%				100%		$1,597,268	29		
factor				85%		$1,879,139	34	-$1,042,026	-21

Annual Savings

Step 4b: Install refined process controls.

The problem with "businesses" and "processes" is that they don't exist, or at least, they only exist in the abstract, as concepts. Fundamentally, businesses are groups of people working together towards a common objective and processes are the habitual routines they follow to "process" the demand customers place on the company. To change a process requires changing the familiar routines people follow in their daily behaviour.

The guiding principle is "show me how you are measured and I will tell you how you behave."

This is an important principle as it links steps **4a** to **4b.** In step **4a** the focus is to reengineer the flow of activity through the business. In step **4b** the focus is to review and reengineer the measures (KPIs) used to manage the processes. Frequently there is no need to change the activity sequence (business process) as it is efficient. Rather change is required in the behaviours associated with the activity sequence in order to remove productivity issues such as pacing and "territory disputes." This change can be achieved, in part or in full, through changing the way the process is measured.

Should the project objective be to specifically review and improve the business processes, then this activity needs to be completed in conjunction with a review of the process measures. This will prevent substantial investment being spent on defining new processes without concurrently establishing the means to drive the necessary behavioural changes.

Steps 5 and 6: Install and drive behavioural change.

The purpose of these steps is to operationalise the agreed changes. To install change is to change behaviour. Occasionally, changing behaviour is straightforward and happens without difficulty. Frequently this is not the case. To mitigate failure, a project requires effective change management.

The **primary purpose** of change management is to assist the company to migrate from a project environment to "business as usual." My observation is that change managers often worry more about completing the standard activities of change management such as communication and training plans, than focusing on the primary purpose.

Strict management of the relationship between **steps 5 and 6** is crucial for a successful project and moving to **step 7**. Measurement is mandatory to reach the highest levels of success at this time. There are two areas of measurement. The first is traditional operational KPIs. These need to be aligned to the future state. This may require changing existing scorecards or even introducing new scorecards.

The second area of measurement should be aligned to the change program itself. The change scorecard should include metrics on skills development and staff attitudes. The intent is to measure both axes in the following matrix.

	Can	Can't
Will	Encourage Role model Use as change leader	On-the-job training Mentor Celebrate achievement
Won't	Counsel Support On-the-job mentoring	Counsel Consider reallocation to other duties

Examples are: number of people trained; number and organisational profile of staff communicated to; number and nature of questions received; survey results; and awareness sessions held.

Step 7: Realise benefits.

This step is the consequence of the prior steps. Success is measured against the business objectives described in the project statement of work and the extended objectives that will have surfaced through the life of the project.

An oft-missed aspect of change is the need to be uncompromising. As the project "gets real" and staff members are asked to change their behaviour, the sponsor will come under significant pressure to relax their position on what success looks like. A culture of "close enough is good enough" is typical at this time. The point here is to emphasize that resistance to change is frequently invisible. It manifests itself in perfectly logical and plausible arguments that are all aimed at reducing the scale of change and the benefits realised. The staff making the arguments may not even realise that they are being resistant to change.

Mitigating resistance to change requires the manager to be aware of the three stages of change:

Stage 1: Mechanical compliance
Stage 2: Conceptual compliance
Stage 3: Utilisation

Source: Proudfoot

Mechanical compliance is characterised by instructing staff to follow the new procedures and being intolerant of reasons as to why it can't be done. As staff become comfortable with the new way of working and establish the new routines of working, they will start to better understand the new order and, if the project has been done well, they will start to see the benefits. They are now at the point of conceptual compliance and once they are comfortable with the benefits of the new procedure they will move to the "utilisation" phase and will own the new way of working. When this happens it can be said that the project has fully migrated to business as usual and the benefits will be realised.

Process Reengineering

I have addressed many of the principles around business process reengineering (BPR) in the previous chapter and in my first book. What will make this chapter different is that it will describe how to prepare for, and run, a BPR workshop and program of improvement. It will repeat a few of the points covered in the previous chapter, as the two chapters are inherently intertwined.

To run a successful BPR project requires context. The easiest way to build context is to establish a table that disaggregates the business from the macro to the micro. Industry language describes this as going from level 1 to level 4. Level 4 is the generic term for the detailed process map, but in practice the disaggregation may drill down to level 5, 6, or 7.

There is no right or wrong, but it is worth considering that if you need to drill down to levels 6 or 7, then you may be narrowing the definition of process too much. This will make it very difficult to keep the process in context.

The disaggregation is represented as follows:

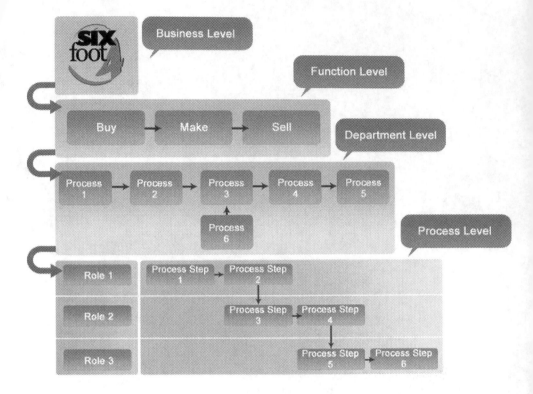

To operationalise this picture prepare a table with the following or similar headers.

ID	lvL 1	Description	lvL 2	Description	lvL 3	Description	lvL 4	Description	Owner	Initiating Process	Exit process	Deliverable	Reports produced	Standard Policy	SLA	KPI
		The purpose of this process is...		The purpose of this process is...		The purpose of this process is...		The purpose of this process is to... It starts with... and ends with...								
								The purpose of this process is to... It starts with... and ends with...								
								The purpose of this process is to... It starts with... and ends with...								
								The purpose of this process is to... It starts with... and ends with...								
								The purpose of this process is to... It starts with... and ends with...								
								The purpose of this process is to... It starts with... and ends with...								
								The purpose of this process is to... It starts with... and ends with...								

The description fields are important as they force the author to think critically about the separation between the processes they are intending to map. It may not be possible to complete all the fields in the first instance. It is recommended that you do not start mapping processes until the data for that process is agreed. Ideally the table will be included in the statement of work.

For the process mapping workshop, you will need a decent size white board, a data projector, and a laptop. The workshop participants should be staff who are very familiar with the process. This may mean that you need more than one "subject matter expert" in the room to adequately cover all aspects of the process.

The following guidelines will add rigour to your process mapping.

1. Model the process using roles not positions.
2. Only one role can be responsible for an activity. Another role can contribute to the activity, but they are not responsible.
3. The input from all trigger processes should be sufficiently consistent with the unit of measure being used in the process. A trigger process is a process that precedes the process you are working on. The output from that process is the input to the next process.

At the very least, the following data should be collected in the workshop, or as a result of the workshop:

- Unit of measure—what is "processed." It provides a means for calculating the annual volume.
- Annual volume—can be broken down to weekly or monthly.
- Process owner.

- Process deliverables/product.
- Distribution list for reports.
- Trigger processes.
- Hand-off processes.
- Roles.
- Indicative role costs.
- Process activities.
- Process sequence.
- Decision points.
- Percentage splits on each decision.
- Work time for each process activity.
- Cycle time for the process.
- Technology used for each activity.

Extended data requirements can include:

- Information gathered at each step.
- Status changes in the item being processed.
- Descriptions of each activity. This may include work instructions.

It is important to establish early on whether you want to draw or model the process. It is almost impossible to adequately collect and evaluate the level of information described above if you do not use process-modelling software. If you use software that only captures the process as a flow sequence, such as Ms Visio, and different software applications such as Ms Word and Excel to capture the additional detail, then you are drawing. In this case you will not be able to complete the analysis described below.

Modelling software allows you to capture the details of the process in the third dimension. That is, you can capture all supporting information in the application at the time of mapping the process. The concept is: write once, use many. There are a range of applications on the market that support this type of process modelling.

To start the workshop, ask the participants to confirm the data collected in the process definition worksheet. Then ask one of the participants to talk you through the process. It is best to have a high-level schema of the process in your head before you start.

Using standard interview techniques, capture the flow sequence on screen in front of everyone. Pay special attention to the words the participants use. Take time to explore inconsistencies or the subtle differences between branches in the flow.

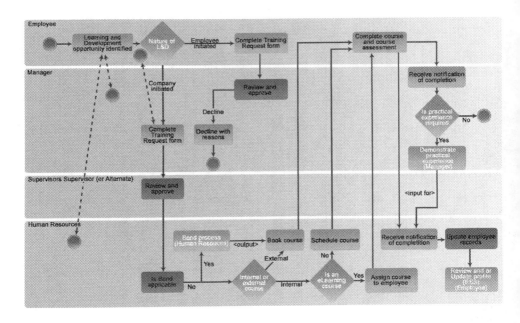

Once you have documented the process, go back through it and capture the required details for each activity. The most important data are the work time for each step, the percentage splits for each decision, and the role costs. With these three data points you can complete the primary process analysis. An additional data point to collect for each activity is the underlying technology and whether it is manual, batch manual or integrated processing.

Please note the following techniques are only possible if you are using modelling software.

For the first round of analysis, use the traditional R.A.C.I. (RACI) (Responsible, Accountable, Contributor, Informed) table.

- The process owner is Accountable.
- The roles are Responsible.
- The distribution list for reports and process outputs helps define who are the Informed stakeholders.
- You may or may not have a Contributor.

The following is an example of a RACI table.

Process / Role	Accounts Payable	Approver	Bank	Cheque Signatories	Corporate Finance Manage
Accounts Payable					
•Generate Vendor AP report on inactive vendors	R				
•Inactive vendors with no activity in last 12 months	R				
End	R			R	R
•Generate Vendor AP report	R				
•Check vendor against Vendor AP report	R				
•Ask requester to complete a vendor setup form	R				
•Complete a vendor request form					
•Update vendor details	R				
•Scan invoice	R				
•Save on F Drive	R				
•Notify of updates required	R				I
•Receive request email and activate vendor					R
•Notify all of completed activation	CI				R
•Process AMEX invoices and staff expenses		A			
•Reminders sent with deadlines for submissions	R				
•Download AMEX transaction statement					
•Attach receipts and statements					
•Update Expenses template					
•Send to Approver		I			
•Code and approve		R			
•Invoices approved		R			

The RACI table allows you to confirm you have gathered all the required information and applied it in the correct manner.

The next level of analysis is to confirm how the process fits into the wider business. That is, do the trigger and hand-off processes make sense? In the graphic below the downward arrows represent trigger processes and the upward arrows are hand-offs. Obviously a hand-off process is also a trigger for the next process. In this way process 1 is the trigger process for process 2 and process 2 is the trigger process for process 3 etc. Each process is measured with KPIs and the relationship between them is measured by SLAs.

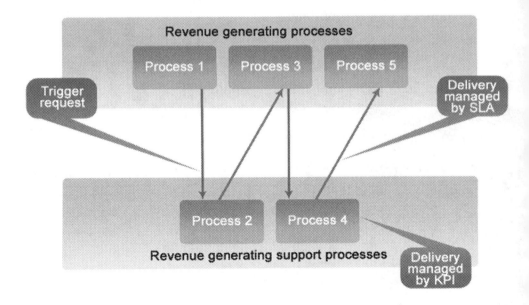

The third level of due diligence is to understand the process data itself. This is done through understanding the sequencing paths within the process.

Consider the following process:

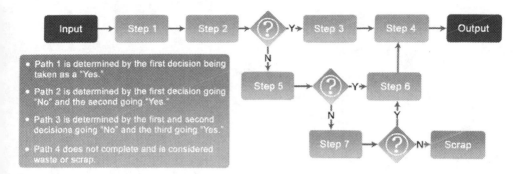

- Path 1 is determined by the first decision being taken as a "Yes."
- Path 2 is determined by the first decision going "No" and the second going "Yes."
- Path 3 is determined by the first and second decisions going "No" and the third going "Yes."
- Path 4 does not complete and is considered waste or scrap.

It is an amalgamation of four paths or processing sequences. The paths are shown as follows:

Path 1

Path 2

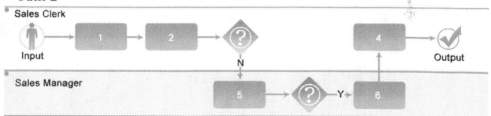

Path 3

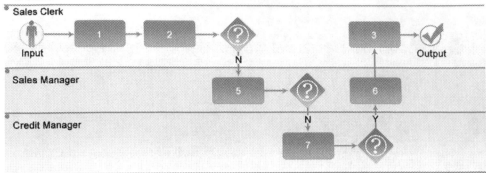

Path 4

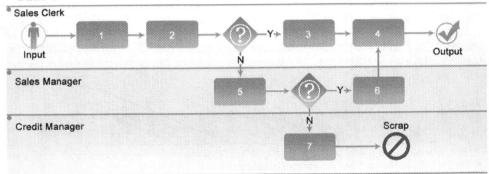

This analysis will produce two key tables:

1. The cost to serve.
2. Full-time equivalents (FTE).

The cost to serve table is shown and provides the weighted average cost for one iteration of the process. This number can be multiplied by the annual volume to get the annual cost.

Path	% of Volume in Path	Activity Based Cost	Weighted Average Cost
1	60	$100	$60
2	20	$200	$40
3	15	$300	$45
4	5	$80	$4
		Total	$149

Column 1 references each way the process can be transacted. In this example there are four paths.

Column 2 is a result of the percentages applied to each decision in the process. (These are not shown in the diagram.)

Column 3 is the activity-based cost of the sum of the activities within each path. The figure is based on the costs associated with each role multiplied by the time associated with each process step in the path.

Column 4 is the product of columns 2 and 3 and represents the cost to serve of one iteration of the process.

The second table is a staffing analysis. It is a similar analysis as is the cost to serve, but is completed on staffing needs-based FTE requirements. The following is an example. It shows FTEs by path and total FTEs for the process for one iteration.

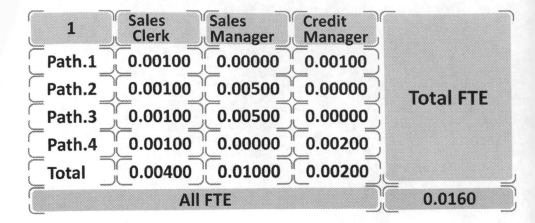

1	Sales Clerk	Sales Manager	Credit Manager	
Path.1	0.00100	0.00000	0.00100	Total FTE
Path.2	0.00100	0.00500	0.00000	
Path.3	0.00100	0.00500	0.00000	
Path.4	0.00100	0.00000	0.00200	
Total	0.00400	0.01000	0.00200	
All FTE				0.0160

The analysis is completed by applying the annual volume to the FTE table. In this case, the annualised staff requirement becomes 1.8 FTEs.

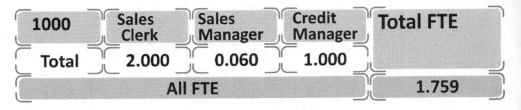

1000	Sales Clerk	Sales Manager	Credit Manager	Total FTE
Total	2.000	0.060	1.000	
All FTE				1.759

Due diligence is to ask: "Does the annualised FTE number make sense? Can the annual volume be completed with 1.8 FTEs?" If you add a productivity factor of 10% or 20% the FTE figure rises to 2 (rounded). If the answer is yes, then you know you have captured the process correctly. If not, then the process data needs to be revisited. The answer does not need to be precise; rather a "substantially correct" answer is accurate enough for decision-making.

Once the individual processes are agreed, they can be aggregated to provide a holistic view. It is the same table as shown in the previous chapter.

The number of variations by which a single item could be processed

The working hours expressed in minutes

The average unit cost

The annual transaction cost for the process

Process by Function	Paths	Unit Time Work (h)	(m)	Elapsed (d)	Unit$	Annual Vol.	C...	FTE	Cost%
BUY									
PURCHASING	14	3.2	194	0.5	$144	3.936	$449,806	7.31	18%
RECEIPTS	28	0.4	26	0.5	$7.79	30,00	$233,700	7.47	9%
ACCOUNTS PAYABLE	63	0.6	35	1.0	$56	2,400	$134,520	0.81	5%
MAKE									
PICKING	18	1.1	68	2.0	$31	8,000	$246,560	5.20	10%
ASSEMBLY	102	1.8	105	2.3	$112	850	$95,591	0.86	4%
DISTRIBUTION	8	1.6	96	4.4	$361	895	$323,096	0.82	13%
INVOICE PROCESSING	17	0.3	15	0.4	$6.57	37,000	$243,090	5.44	10%
SELL									
CATALOGUES	14	25.0	1500	10.0	$51	6	$305	0.09	0%
MARKETING	3	6.0	360	30.0	$18.99	1,000	$18,990	3.45	1%
INVOICE PROCESSING	7	0.5	30	1.0	$18	100	$1,717	0.03	0%
IT MANAGEMENT									
USER ACCESS CONTROL	12	0.3	15	4.0	$7.80	25,000	$195,000	3.59	8%
ENQUIRY MANAGEMENT	11	0.9	56	0.2	$53	1,936	$102,724	1.04	4%
NEW USER SETUP	18	0.5	30	4.0	$20	21,600	$437,832	6.21	18%
					P%	0%	$2,482,990	42.30	100%
					factor	%	$2,921,165	50	

Elapsed times are very conservative. Lower end estimates have been used throughout.

The average days elapsed to process a volume of 1 (drives customer service)

The annual transaction volume through this process

The full time equivalent staff requirement

With this table, process improvement can be prioritised. Assuming the intent is to reduce costs, you read the right-hand column. It shows the relative contribution of the individual process costs to the sum of costs for all processes. It can be seen that the "purchasing" and "new user setup" are the two processes that contribute most to total costs.

To reduce the costs associated with a business process refer to the cost to serve table.

Path	% of Volume in Path	Activity Based Cost	Weighted Average Cost
1	60	$100	$60
2	20	$200	$40
3	15	$300	$45
4	5	$80	$4
		Total	$149

Path 1 is the most cost-effective processing sequence. The best outcome is to reengineer the process to maximise the volume flowing through this path. This will deliver a savings of $49 per process iteration. If the process is transacted 10000 times a year, then this is a savings of $490,000. If you cannot improve the process to get 100% through path 1, then the next best option is to maximise volume through path 1 and use path 2 for the overflow.

Moving 100% of the volume to path 1 can be achieved through controlling the decision.

Typically this can be achieved through a change to the:

1. Staff profile through skills improvement or behavioural change.
2. Processing sequence through policy or procedural changes.
3. Underlying technology through workflows and configuring the existing system.

A change in skills will require further analysis to be able to answer the questions illustrated below.

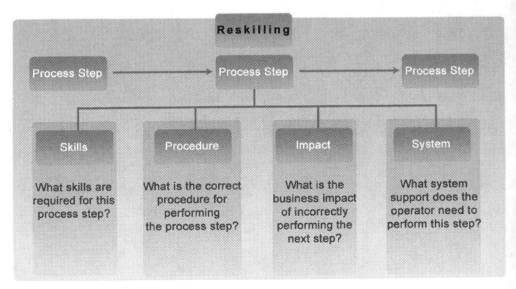

The approach is to complete this analysis for each step in the process and then aggregate them into a consolidated table. This table can be cross-referenced to the RACI table to check for completeness. Once this data is collected, it can be cross-referenced to the skill profile of the staff working in the process and improvement strategies developed.

Option 3 is the best option as the application of technology or a workflow removes the option for the process performer to make a decision in the process. This concept is explored further in the chapter on Judgement Support and Decision-Making.

Recognising that this type of process change is frequently quite substantial in its nature, it is better to complete the analysis for all processes as shown in the following table and then develop a business improvement program to meet the change requirements of all processes at once.

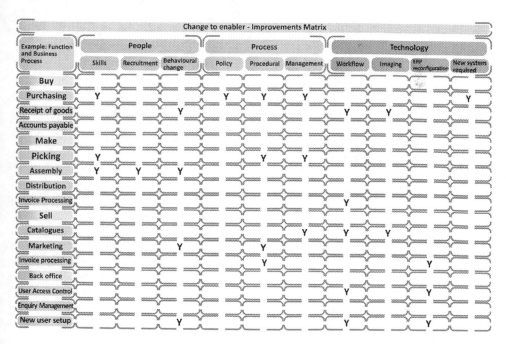

Change to enabler - Improvements Matrix

Example: Function and Business Process	People			Process			Technology			
	Skills	Recruitment	Behavioural change	Policy	Procedural	Management	Workflow	Imaging	ERP reconfiguration	New system required
Buy										
Purchasing	Y			Y	Y	Y				Y
Receipt of goods			Y				Y	Y		
Accounts payable										
Make										
Picking	Y				Y	Y				
Assembly	Y	Y	Y							
Distribution										
Invoice Processing							Y			
Sell										
Catalogues						Y	Y	Y		
Marketing			Y		Y					
Invoice processing					Y				Y	
Back office										
User Access Control							Y		Y	
Enquiry Management										
New user setup			Y				Y		Y	

Before implementation commences it is important that the business case for change is validated. The above table identifies the entire program of required improvements and these improvements are then used to recalculate all tables described throughout this chapter. The expected benefits are then compared to the existing process metrics.

		Current Mode of Operation								
		Unit Time				Annual				
		Work	Elapsed							
Process by Function	Paths	(h)	(m)	(d)	Unit$	Vol.	Cost	FTE	Cost%	
BUY										
PURCHASING	14	3.2	194	0.5	$144	3.936	$449,806	7.31	18%	
RECEIPTS	28	0.4	26	0.5	$7.79	30,00	$233,700	7.47	9%	
ACCOUNTS PAYABLE	63	0.6	35	1.0	$56	2,400	$134,520	0.81	5%	
MAKE										
PICKING	18	1.1	68	2.0						
ASSEMBLY	102	1.8	105	2.3						
DISTRIBUTION	8	1.6	96	4.4						
INVOICE PROCESSING	17	0.3	15	0.4						
SELL										
CATALOGUES	14	25.0	1500	10.0						
MARKETING	3	6.0	360	30.0						
INVOICE PROCESSING	7	0.5	30	1.0						
IT MANAGEMENT										
USER ACCESS CONTROL	12	0.3	15	4.0						
ENQUIRY MANAGEMENT	11	0.9	56	0.2						
NEW USER SETUP	18	0.5	30	4.0						

		Future Mode of Operation							
		Unit Time				Annual		Change	
		Work	Elapsed						
Paths	(h)	(m)	(d)	Unit$	Vol.	Cost	FTE	Cost	FTE
4	1.7	102.7	0.4	$62	3.936	244,032	3.87	-$205,744	-3
7	0.3	15.6	0.3	$4	30,00	$120,000	4.48	-$113,700	-3
12	0.4	24.5	0.5	$18	2,400	$43,200	0.56	-$91,320	0
12	0.4	24.0	0.5	$16	8,000	$128,000	1.84	-$118,560	-3
16	0.9	52.7	1.5	$49	850	$41,650	0.43	-$53,941	0
5	1.0	60.0	2.0	$96	895	$87,710	0.51	-$235,385	0
4	0.2	10.8	0.1	$4	37,000	$148,000	3.81	-$95,090	-2
4	0.8	45.0	3.0	$43	10,800	$464,400	4.66	-$464,095	-5
3	3.0	180.0	10	$12	1,000	$12,000	1.72	-$5,990	-2
2	0.1	8.0	0.4	$7	100	$700	0.01	-$1,077	0
4	0.0	1.0	0.1	$2	25,000	$39,000	0.24	-$156,000	-3
4	0.5	31.4	0.1	$16	1,936	$30,976	0.58	-$71,748	0
6	0.5	31.7	0.2	$11	21,600	$237,600	6.55	-$200,232	0
				P%	100%	$1,597,268	29		
				factor	85%	$1,879,139	34	-$1,042,026	-21
								Annual Savings	

In this example, a total benefit of more than one million has been identified with an associated saving of 21 FTEs. The nature of these 21 FTEs can be identified through a comparison of the staff profile tables.

FTE By Internal Role - Current Mode of Operation

Process	Role 1	Role 2	Role 3	Role 4	Role 5	Role 6	Role 7	Role 8	Role 9	Role 10	Role 11	Role 12	Total FTE
Buy													
Purchasing		2.0				1.3	2.9	0.70	0.330				7.26
Receipts						2.00	4.0	0.16		1.00	0.300		7.46
Accounts payable			0.5				0.3						0.77
Make													
Picking					1.7		2.0		0.6				
Assembly													
Distribution									0.8				
Invoice Processing						0.6							
Sell													
Catalogues		0.1											
Marketing	1.4	2.0											
Invoice processing				0.1		0.2							
IT management													
User Access Control	3.6												
Enquiry management	1.0												
New user setup	6.2												
	1.4	12.8	2.1	0.6	1.7	5.0	9.2	0.86	1.8				

FTE By Internal Role - Future Mode of Operation

Process	Role 1	Role 2	Role 3	Role 4	Role 5	Role 6	Role 7	Role 8	Role 9	Role 10	Role 11	Role 12	Total FTE
Buy													
Purchasing		1.60				0.68	1.01	0.37	0.17				3.84
Receipts							1.20	2.40	0.08		0.60	0.18	4.48
Accounts payable				0.33				0.21					0.54
Make													
Picking						0.68	0.29	0.54		0.21			1.83
Assembly									0.43				0.43
Distribution										0.51			0.51
Invoice Processing							0.42			2.60	0.28	0.28	3.78
Sell													
Catalogues			3.63										3.63
Marketing	0.70		1.10										1.80
Invoice processing					0.27		0.64						0.90
IT management													
User Access Control		0.24											0.24
Enquiry management		0.58											0.59
New user setup		6.52											6.52
	0.7	8.9	4.7	0.6	0.7	3.2	4.3	0.9	0.9	3.4	0.6	0.3	28.0

I close with the following comments. Business process reengineering is reasonably straightforward to do at the "surface" level, and somewhat more difficult to do at the detailed level. A schematic of a process is just that—a schematic. It is a representation of the routines staff follow on a daily basis and to reengineer the process requires a change in these routines. To gain the trust of the affected staff requires a rigorous analysis of the processes combined with a focused program of change management. It is equally important to remember that processes do not exist in isolation and to change a process without understanding how the process interfaces with the rest of the business is likely to reduce the overall benefits received.

Swatting the S.W.O.T.

The S.W.O.T (SWOT) analysis is a staple model in any self-respecting business analyst's kitbag and specifically those in the strategy function. As the acronym indicates, the purpose of the SWOT is to determine the Strengths and Weaknesses within the business and the Opportunities and Threats posed by the external environment.

These terms can stand alone but the synergies between them drive real insights. Example: Strengths and Threats are closely aligned. This does not mean that for every strength there must be a corresponding threat. It does mean that if you consider one aspect of the business a strength, then it is wise to seriously consider what's happening in the market that could challenge that strength.

For example, about eight years ago, I was facilitating a two-day offsite workshop with a group of senior managers. They argued strongly that their primary competitive advantage was that their call centre was "in-country." I suggested that the telecommunications market was already changing and call centres were moving offshore and becoming a commodity service.

They refused to accept this point and said their product was reliant on having an in-country service. I pointed out that they already serviced New Zealand from Australia, but they said that was different. They now use a call centre from offshore. They were forced to, as the threat they originally denied has almost become the standard go-to service for all players in their market.

The four quadrants of the SWOT are typically drawn up in a 2 by 2 grid.

The truth is that I seldom ever see a SWOT that I consider to be worth the paper it is written on. The inadequacies are threefold:

1. The content lacks context.
2. There is no obvious answer to the "so what?" question and
3. The content is frequently riddled with motherhood statements.

A motherhood statement is a statement that makes little or no sense in the negative. By way of example, I Googled "SWOT Analysis" and picked the first result, which you can see in the graphic.

SWOT Analysis

Strengths
- Technological skills
- Leading brands
- Distribution channels
- Customer Loyalty/Relationship
- Production quality
- Scale
- Management

Weaknesses
- Absence of important skills
- Weak brands
- Poor access to distribution
- Low customer retention
- Unreliable product/service
- Sub-scale
- Management

Internal factors

Opportunities
- Changing customer tastes
- Technological advances
- Changes in government politics
- Lower personal taxes
- Change in population age
- New distribution channels

Threats
- Changing customer base
- Closing of geographic markets
- Technological advances
- Changes in government politics
- Tax increases
- Change in population age
- New distribution channels

External factors

Positive   **Negative**

From Agrowiki. http://argowiki.com/images/2/26/SWOT_analysis_example.png

If you look at "Strengths," the first line is technological skills. This is a great example of a motherhood statement. What does it mean? Try to state it in the negative. You could go for "no technological skills" but what if the intended strength was "unique technological skills" or perhaps it was referring to a situation where the company had done away with the need for technological skills. If the negative of the statement cannot be easily articulated then the positive should be considered equally nonsensical.

Additionally using a 2 by 2 grid tends to limit thinking and divorce the authors from the intended scope of the SWOT analysis. The author frequently captures the obvious statements and once they have a handful of statements for each header they stop. The graphic is a good example of this point.

To address these issues I recommend overlaying the SWOT analysis against the process being analysed. At the highest level, the process is the value chain.

Inbound Logistics	Operations	Outbound Logistics	Sales and Marketing	Service

Other processes could be the procure to pay, order to cash or a detailed process such as warehouse management.

Using the value chain the SWOT would look as follows:

	Inbound Logistics	Operations	Outbound Logistics	Sales and Marketing	Service
Strengths					
Weaknesses					
Opportunities					
Threats					

Now take the strength of "technological skills." Where would you apply it? Or take the weakness of "sub scale." Where would you apply it (whatever it means)?

Once you have completed the analysis, review it for empty cells. Does an empty cell mean there is genuinely no content for that cell or does it mean that the authors have not thought hard enough about it?

Using this layout, you can prepare a meaningful analysis without using statements.

	Inbound Logistics	Operations	Outbound Logistics	Sales and Marketing	Service
Strengths	●	●	●	●	●
Weaknesses	●	●	●	●	●
Opportunities	●	●	●	●	●
Threats	●	●	●	●	●

Dark is weak. Light is strong.

Visually it is readily obvious that the company has a problem in Inbound Logistics, Operations and Sales and Marketing. The strength is in Outbound Logistics followed by Service.

Finally the "so what?" question must be answered. If you look at the Agrowiki SWOT graphic, it is impossible to draw a meaningful conclusion from the analysis. If you look at the SWOT analysis in association with the value chain, it is substantially easier to draw meaningful conclusions from the analysis.

There are no right or wrong answers when working with models. But there are stronger and weaker analyses. Giving a model context will always produce a stronger result. Here's wishing you all the best with your future modelling.

Draw the Picture

Two of the biggest difficulties in the work environment are a) being able to quickly understand and contextualise difficult concepts and then b) being able to convey these complex concepts to colleagues or managers. These skills are almost mandatory for uninterrupted career advancement.

There have been many studies on the way people assimilate knowledge and no one shoe fits all. Depending on who you are you will prefer written text, audio, or graphics. My view is that if you can't draw it, you don't fully understand it. A graphic forces you to summarise your thinking, to organize it tightly into a visual object. Both written and spoken words allow you to describe the same concept from a few different angles and to really elaborate on the idea. A picture is static. Everything you want to say has to be summarised in the graphic and you are limited by the size of the page.

To get a picture right means that you really have to understand the concept you are drawing and the interrelationships within it.

There is no right or wrong way to draw a picture. You can use blocks and lines, symbols or a mind map. Once you get the picture right, you will be able to talk to it for an extended period of time.

Sometime back I was wrestling with how strategy was related to a business. I drew the following picture.

I look at the picture today and while I still agree with it, there are parts of it I would change. But at the time I drew it, that was how I understood the world. It summarised a few hundred pages of text. Once I had the picture clear in my head I was confident that I could take any question on the topic and be able to answer it in detail and in the context of how it worked with the rest of the business.

There is no formal methodology for drawing a picture and you need to be patient with yourself. It may take a few days to get the picture to a point where you are comfortable with it.

The underlying assumption of this approach is that any message you receive, be it a written text, a verbal instruction or lecture, or even a visual event will only contain a half dozen important points. It is these points that you must include in your picture. The trick is identifying the points in the first place. My recommendation is: don't try too hard. Use an A4 size piece of paper and draw your understanding of what you have just read or heard or seen. Make the picture rich in detail. The more detail, the better. Once you believe you have all the concepts on the page and you have related them to each other, take a new A4 and fold it in half. Now draw the same picture in half the space. It will force you to summarise your first picture. If you can, repeat the exercise with a one-quarter size piece of paper.

Then reverse the process. When you can draw the summarised picture from memory, then draw the next level of expanded picture and when you have that right, draw the very detailed picture again. When you can do that, then you will find you really have internalised the concepts and you will be able to talk about them fluently. Then, depending on who your audience is, you can produce the appropriately summarised picture on the white board without notes and speak to it with confidence.

The following is another example of a picture I have used for years to describe the business architecture.

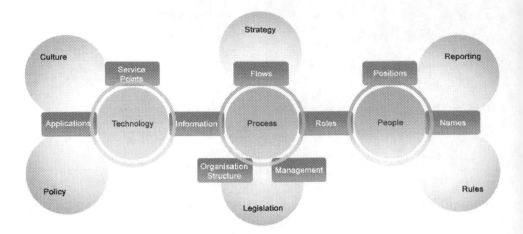

This picture conveys a significant amount of detail without being overly busy. It describes the elements of the business architecture and the context in which they exist. I now know this picture so well I can speak to it for over an hour if needed. I have also prepared pictures for each of the nine points (shown as blocks). This allows me to drill down into additional detail if necessary.

I have mentored a number of entrepreneurs who have come to me with an idea and the passion to start a business. They will all have prepared detailed business plans, but when asked to describe their idea they invariably battle. My recommendation is always: write up a brochure of one page only with a picture. The potential client must be able to look at the picture and understand your business. The text is supporting detail only. When you can do that, you understand what you are selling.

It is said, a picture speaks a thousand words. This is true and when you have your picture, you will have a thousand words at your fingertips.

Surveys and Diagnostics

There is a significant body of management science behind the formation, delivery, management, and interpretation of surveys, sufficient to fill a series of books in its own right. The intent of this article is only to provide the layperson with some guidelines for preparing and administering a survey, suitable for use within the company or the customer base.

There are three truths that underpin any change initiative. The first two are:

1. If you can tell me how you are measured, I will show you how you behave. The principle is that measurement drives behaviour.
2. People only change when their discomfort is high, caused by "pain" or unrealised "pleasure." These two points are on opposite ends of the spectrum. If people are experiencing any point in between, then they are unlikely to change.

A survey is a quick and easy means to measure both points with the second being easier to measure than the first. The most important feature of a survey is that it is only a snapshot of people's perceptions at a specific point in time. This brings me to the third truth:

3. General statements do not define the specific and the specific does not define general statements.

A survey provides a snapshot in time on general statements only. For example, a survey on customer satisfaction may indicate that customers are highly satisfied with the service they have received. This does not mean that every single customer is happy and it would not be difficult to find a single customer who was unhappy. All you can conclude from the survey is that generally customers are happy. Equally, just because you found one customer that was unhappy, that does not invalidate the survey.

The biggest mistake in surveys is measuring what you cannot change. This issue typically manifests itself through broad questions. The less specific the question, the more it is open to interpretation by the respondent. Consider the question: "Are you happy? Answer yes or no." This may seem like a specific question due to the binary nature of the answer, but it is actually a very general question. What is "happy?" How do I know when I am happy, or do I measure my happiness the same way as the next person?

Assume a 60/40 split in responses, yes to no. At best, given the inherent vagueness in the concept of happiness, the most reliable insight that can be inferred from the study, is that, at the time of answering the question, 60% of the respondents were not unhappy. It does not predict if the same people will be happy one minute or one hour later. If your objective was to make everyone happy, then this survey offers no insight into what is making people happy or unhappy. It provides no clue as to what needs to change. In summary, this style of question is a waste of time.

A better approach is break the concept you wish to measure into its component parts, ensuring that no matter what the answer, you will be able to introduce a change that will improve the result. Assume you wish to survey management's perception of the quality of information they receive. The first hurdle is to define the concept of "quality." As per the happiness example, it would be futile to ask management if they considered the information they received to be of poor or good quality, as you would not know what to change if the answer was that the quality of the information was poor.

To resolve this issue, I define quality information to be information that is complete, accurate, and timely. In other words, I get all the information I want, when I want it and without errors.

Using this definition the first question could be: "Do you consider the information you receive to be complete?" It is substantially easier to resolve issues around incomplete information than it is to fix issues of poor quality. A further refinement of the question can be to ask "How often are you required to request additional information for use in the decision-making process?" as it may not be possible to be confident that everyone defines "complete" the same way.

The survey is further improved by moving away from using binary answers (yes/no) to using a scale. A scale allows the respondent to be more specific in their answers. The Likert scale is my preference. The primary characteristic of a Likert scale is that it considers all responses to be equal. To set it up, the survey author should write down the question and then, at a minimum, define each side of the scale. Ideally each response point in the scale will also be labelled.

A Likert scale should comprise at least five choices. The ideal number is eight as it allows the respondent to show a higher sensitivity in how they respond to each question. I prefer using an even number of choices as it forces a decision from the respondent. Using an odd number provides a natural midpoint that can become the easy choice for respondents not wishing to commit themselves. There is no midpoint with an even number of choices.

The question on completeness now looks like this:

How often are you required to request additional information for use in the decision-making process?

Constantly							Seldom
1	2	3	4	5	6	7	8

The results are presented by totalling the number of times each point is selected, as each point on the scale is equally valid.

I also recommend asking the question twice. The first question is to evaluate the current position and the second is to determine the ideal or desired position.

The results graph could look as follows:

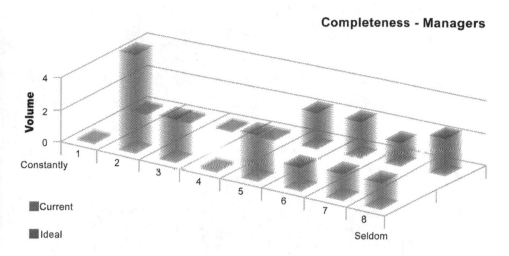

The current position is in front and the ideal position at the back.

From the graph it can be seen that of the 110 respondents (managers within the business), 40 rated the current completeness of information as 2, 20 rated it with a 3, 0 rated it with a 4, 20 rated it with a 5 and 10 rated it for each of 6, 7 and 8.

The important point is that there is no trend line. It is only a series of discrete scores.

From the graph it can be extrapolated that 50% of managers consider the information they receive to be incomplete. This is an easily accepted result. What is unexpected is that 60% of managers have an ideal score of 5 and 6. That is, over half of the survey population did not consider it important to have complete information to do their jobs.

These results can be further enhanced with follow-up interviews to better understand them.

And further insight can be gained through cross-referencing their responses to the demographic information about the respondents such as seniority, gender, location, function etc.

Once you have established the gap between the current and the ideal position, the question of how to close it arises. My experience is that the gaps are closed through a combination of changes to policy, behaviour, process and technology. The following table illustrates how this can be worked through:

Attribute	Behaviour	Policy	Process	Technology
Measure 1	1		3	2
Measure 2	2	3	1	4
Measure 3	2	4	1	3
Measure 4		1		
Measure 5	4	3	2	1
Measure 6		1		
Measure 7		1		
Measure 8		1		
Measure 9	3	4	1	2
Measure 10	1		3	2

On the left are the criteria measured by the survey. On the right are the four change drivers of behaviour, policy, process, and technology. The numbers represent which of the four drivers need to be addressed to close the gap and are in decreasing order of priority. (1 is highest priority and 4 lowest.)

It can be seen that substantial improvements across all measures can be made by changing or introducing policy supplemented by changes to behaviour and process. Frequently companies jump straight to changes to technology. In this case, changes to technology will help, but they are not the place to start.

A survey can act as a catalyst for change and can provide a baseline prior to making changes. But it is important to keep in mind that it is only a snapshot in time and it only provides answers to the specific questions that you ask.

Judgement Support and Decision-making

To make a decision you need information and you can only make a decision about the present or the future. Making a decision about how to handle a past event is still a decision about the future.

Information has six attributes. It must be relevant, accurate, timely, supported, accessible, and complete.

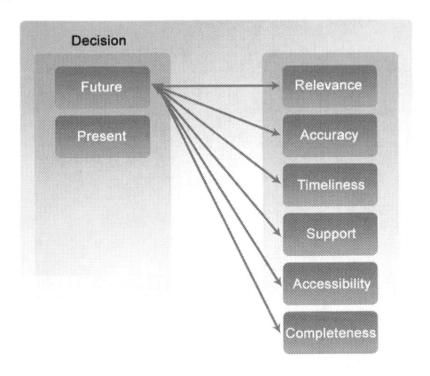

Different personality types will make a decision based on different percentages of information. A good decision-maker will make a decision when the time is right, even if they have incomplete information, as long as the information they do have is relevant, accurate, and accessible. These types of people are rare. More frequently, organisations get bogged down as the business waits for decisions to be made and the decision-makers request an ever-increasing amount of information.

Getting the decision right is important because bad decision-making is the most expensive activity in a business. Not making a decision is equally expensive.

The question therefore becomes: "How do you accelerate decision-making whilst devolving it to the lower levels of management yet still maintaining the quality of the decisions made?" One way to do this is to provide the manager with pre-vetted decisions. This way they only need to use their judgement about which decision best fits a specific set of circumstances. This could substantially reduce expenses in a business, but for most businesses this is wishful thinking.

The concept of judgement support was first introduced to me by Russell Swanborough. He explained that decision support is the process of providing information to assist in decision-making. Judgement support is the process of providing a selection of suitable decisions for a manager to choose from in order to find the best one for the specific business circumstances.

Industries that get judgement support right are those that use statistics as a core competency, for example, insurance companies. If you call up an insurance company and ask for cover they will vet your profile against the "bell curve" and offer you cover accordingly. They take almost zero interest in you as an individual and the call centre operator cannot make a decision on your personal circumstances. All they can do is guide you through the screening process and then offer you predefined choices of cover. They can use their judgement as to which cover is best for you.

To implement judgement support into the lower levels of the business requires the business to know what decisions are being made in the first place.

There are two types of decisions that get made in a business where judgement support can be applied. The first is before a process starts and the second is at each decision point within the process.

Consider the following process.

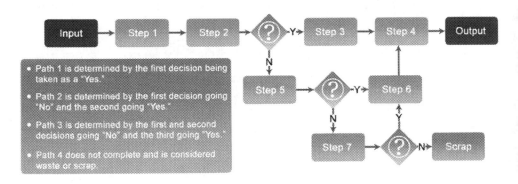

The process has three decisions in it. Each decision creates a different path and each path has a different cost to serve. Consider the following table.

Path	% of Volume in Path	Activity Based Cost	Weighted Average Cost
1	60	$100	$60
2	20	$200	$40
3	15	$300	$45
4	5	$80	$4
		Total	$149

Following path 1 is the most cost-effective processing sequence. It also carries the highest volume.

Path 1 is shown.

Every time the sales clerk transacts the process they are faced with the same decision. Depending on the decision they make, the cost of the process either remains at $100 or increases to $200 or $300 or, worse, the process is not completed at all.

A bad decision is therefore an expensive decision. To mitigate bad decisions the sale clerk could be given a set of parameters to which they would have to adhere. They can make any decision they like as long as it is within these parameters. The assumption is that the suite of decisions that make up the parameters is known and accepted and would always ensure path 1 is followed, irrespective of the particular decision made.

If they wished to move the sale down path 2, then they would require approval, or they may have to ensure the sales process meets a more rigorous set of sales parameters.

The idea is to recognise that the decision is a key point in the process in that it directly impacts gross margin. Making the wrong decision could result in the sale losing money.

The other point in the process where judgement support can be applied is at the start. Before the process is triggered, the supervisor can use their judgement to commence work or not. If the process cannot be completed on path 1, then it may be preferable not to start work at all. The supervisor should be provided with clear criteria about when to commence work and when to pause the process. They then use their judgement to evaluate if the incoming work meets either criterion. What they can't do is to decide that they will commence work anyway, knowing that it cannot complete for whatever reason.

Technology can also be used to implement judgement support. Solution sets such as Business Process Management can be configured to ensure the process follows the "bouncing ball." This means that the process worker has to deal with the screens in the order that they are presented. Any decision they will need to make should have already been configured into the process and it is predetermined when those decisions will present themselves. Only at these times can the process worker use their own judgement as to the best way to proceed.

Saving the Team

One of the great projects I had the opportunity to work on was the IBM consultancy to Mercedes-Benz South Africa. The project managers did everything right. At the start of the project they took the time to properly establish a project team comprising of MBSA and IBM staff. This included classroom training for the team to ensure a common approach, team-building activities and engaging with the client. This foundation ensured that the project was enjoyable and rewarding. The hours were long as is normal on a consultancy but nobody seemed to mind.

The end of my involvement on the project correlated well with my move to Australia. I made the final recommendations presentation to the MBSA executive team and two days later I moved to Australia. The presentation had gone very well and I was on a high.

Once I found my feet in Australia, I reapplied to IBM to join the local consulting practice. My application was accepted and I was soon on the projects. The problem was that the projects were not MBSA. The teams were new, the objectives were different, and the project culture was different. In short I was unhappy and I quit. On the MBSA project I had been part of a high-performing team, established over months of focused project work. I mourned for what I had left behind.

As a consultant you are expected to move from project to project without difficulty, and I do it today without thought. What made the MBSA experience different is that I left it at the high point. I had delivered a successful final presentation and walked out of the boardroom, out of IBM and out of the country. I took no time to celebrate success with my colleagues. No time to debrief from the project and no time to bring closure to my role.

My experience provided me with firsthand practical insight into Dr. Bruce Tuckman's model on teaming.

Dr. Bruce Tuckman published his "Forming Storming Norming Performing" model in 1965. He added a fifth stage, "Adjourning," in the 1970s. Tuckman's model explains that as a team develops maturity and ability, relationships establish, and the leader changes leadership style to further the team's evolution. He or she begins with a directing style, moves through coaching, then participating, then finishes delegating and ends with a style that is almost detached. At this point the team may produce a successor leader and the previous leader can move on to develop a new team.

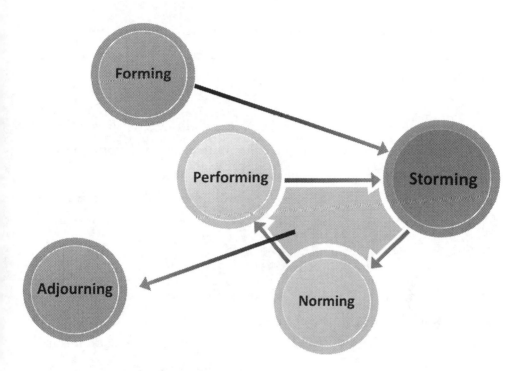

The adjourning stage is also referred to as the mourning stage, when team members mourn for the high performance "hellfire" days of the project and the camaraderie of the project team.

This final phase is frequently not recognised as important or, at best, is poorly managed. As professionals, managers are expected to "just deal with it" and keep their problems to themselves. As I found, this is not that easy.

Once I had lived the experience, I began to see it all around me. I met many senior executives who were put in charge of large business improvement projects within their company, and who resigned after the project completed. Not immediately after the project, but within a reasonably short time of the project end. For the company, this is a problem, as frequently these projects are part of the manager's succession plan.

The more I saw it, the more I took an active interest in the problem and, through discussion and observation, concluded that the primary cause was one of exposure.

Prior to commencing the project, a manager will have been working in their normal role, dealing with the daily routine expected from that role. They would have known where the role started and ended and what the limits of their authority were. They would be diplomatic with their colleagues, preferring to worry about their own role and allowing others to do the same in theirs.

When the manager is taken out of their routine and placed in a senior project role, the rules change. No longer are they confined to the boundaries of their position. No longer do the rules of business diplomacy prevent them from enquiring about why their colleagues are doing what they are doing; in fact, they are now expected to investigate the way their colleagues work.

Driving a large business improvement project gives them licence to ask questions of the company and to review material they would not typically see in their daily role. Through the project they are exposed to the "soul" of the company. They are exposed to the inadequacies of the senior managers. When you look into the soul of a company, you cannot forget, you cannot "un-see" what you have seen. You cannot go back. The firm assumption that senior managers know what they are doing becomes less firm.

As a project lead, they are expected to think strategically and consider the big picture. This can be vastly different from their previous role as a silo manager.

When the project is over, it is almost impossible for the manager to return to their old position. They have just spent six months or more working harder, longer, and with more freedom than they ever had before. They have had almost unlimited access to the executive team.

In short, they are no longer the same employee as they were when they started the project and it is foolhardy to expect them to forget and return to the comparatively bland existence of their previous routine. If they are asked to, they quit.

There is an equally dark flip side to this issue. As the manager grows in confidence through the project and develops their insights into the company, they become a threat to more senior management who don't want their "dirty washing" exposed and don't want the manager getting ahead of themselves. The end result is that the manager is forced out of the company.

To address the issue and to save the skills within the company, senior executives need to create a new role for the manager coming off the project. Invariably this requires that the company find or create a suitably senior role that allows the manager to come "back into" the company whilst respecting the journey of discovery the manager went through over the course of the project. It is important to recognise that the manager who led the project is not a professional project manager and frequently they wish to keep their line management career intact.

The same issues exist for more junior staff members seconded to projects to work with consultants, either as subject matter experts or as a general project resource. These employees are also exposed to company details they would not normally see and witness or participate in conversations with the consultants that discuss the failings of the company. Under the influence of this often negative messaging, they start to see their managers in a different light. They will also start to work longer hours than their colleagues. As an individual, they will grow in confidence and as part of a team, they start to "perform."

Project staff do not expect to get promoted when a project ends, but they do expect to be recognised for their contribution and to this end it is important to hold structured celebratory events to recognise the project and individual efforts. Failure to recognise an individual's contribution will almost certainly cause the staff member to become disillusioned with the company. They will feel as if they have become an expendable commodity and not a valuable contributor to the company.

It is unlikely that they will resign, but it reasonable to expect that they will be less engaged with the company. This feeling of isolation can be amplified if the project has caused them to drift apart from their colleagues. Before they could gossip and share information. Now that they have had access to confidential information, they cannot share information and invariably this creates distance between themselves and their colleagues.

There is no easy remedy for this problem. The most successful mitigation strategy is to agree the post-project role description for the employee before the project starts. The new role should stretch the employee more than the project did. In this way they will rely on skills they learnt through the project and will not have time to mourn the end of the project. Done well, the employee will hardly notice the change.

An equally viable strategy and similar to the above, is to ensure the employee has a structured succession or career development plan in place. This plan should supersede the project enabling the employee to contextualise the project as part of their greater development program. In this case, it is expected that the employee will come off the project requiring less structured support for their re-assimilation into the business-as-usual routine. Their period of mourning should be reduced but it is unlikely to be removed altogether.

Both of these strategies will be of immense benefit if the company works with the consultancy from the beginning to agree how the consultants should develop the employee. This will includes activities such as allowing the employee to deliver important presentations through the course of the project.

In closing, I note that the above observations and strategies are general in their nature and will assist executives and managers to retain staff, but when it comes to human nature, each person is different and has different needs. Those staff who are in "deep mourning" will require a re-assimilation strategy personalised to their specific needs.